Texas Eminent Domain Condemnation Guide

What To Do When They Want Your Land

David Todd
Attorney at Law

If the government or a corporation wants to take your land for a public project, this guide is for you. Learn how Texas eminent domain condemnation works and how to protect your rights and get the compensation you deserve. David Todd and the Todd Law Firm protect commercial and large-tract landowners in condemnation cases across Texas.

This guide does not constitute legal advice or create an attorney-client relationship. You should consult an eminent domain attorney to discuss the specifics of your case.

For a free review of your situation and to learn how we can help protect your rights as a landowner, call us now at **(512) 472-7799** or visit **davidtoddlaw.com**.

Copyright 2020 by David W. Todd.
All rights reserved.

1. Introduction:
   A Crash Course in Condemnation   p.5

2. Understanding Eminent Domain:
   Why They Can Take Your Land   p.7

3. The Condemnation Process:
   A Step-by-Step Flowchart   p.8

4. Condemnation Steps:
   The Details   p.10

5. Right-of-Way Agents:
   Tricks of the Trade   p.17

6. Terms of an Easement:
   Look Beyond the Money   p.21

7. The Condemnation Appraiser:
   An Essential Investment   p.24

8. Special Commissioners' Hearing:
   A Unique Aspect of Condemnation   p.27

9. Hire a Condemnation Lawyer:
   Your Key to Success   p.30

10. How We Can Help:
    Why You Should Contact Us Now   p. 33

1.
Introduction:
A Crash Course in Condemnation

A very nice couple worked hard all their lives and used part of what they earned to buy a small ranch in north Texas. The ranch was their getaway spot from the hectic pace of their big city home, a place to clear their heads, get back to their small-town roots, work the land and relax. One day they got a letter saying that a giant company planned to run 80-foot tall electric power line towers across their property, ruining the beauty of their land. They were angry, frustrated and unsure what to do. They wondered: how could a company just come and take their land?

They called their son, the only lawyer in the family, for help. For him, this was the beginning of a crash course in how to fight for landowners when a corporation or the government wants to take private land for a public project using the power of "eminent domain." After a lot of hard work, their son was able to get them much more compensation than the company initially offered. He was also able to protect their rights by insisting on the best possible terms for the agreement.

That couple with the ranch was my parents and I was the "lawyer son" they called. I enjoyed helping my folks fight this project and get a great result. As a result, I decided to dedicate myself to helping landowners get full compensation and fair treatment in eminent domain condemnation cases.

When your land may be taken through eminent domain, the more you know the better you can protect your rights and make sure you are treated fairly. Reading this guide is your first step to winning your condemnation case.

2.
Understanding Eminent Domain:
Why They Can Take Your Land

The government's right to take private property for public use is implied in the constitutions of both Texas and the United States. The Fifth Amendment to the United States Constitution states "...nor shall private property be taken for public use, without just compensation." The Texas Constitution states "No person's property may be taken, damaged, or destroyed for or applied to public use without adequate compensation." Note that both constitutions require that fair payment must be made to the property owner by whichever entity is taking their land. A private organization like a corporation can gain the same eminent domain authority as the government if they intend to use the land for a public project and if they follow the proper procedures.

"**Eminent domain**" is the authority of the government or a private entity to take private property for public use.

"**Condemnation**" refers to the legal procedure the government or a company must follow when exercising eminent domain authority to force the sale of a landowner's private property. An entity with eminent domain authority to start condemnation proceedings may be referred to as the "condemning authority", "condemning entity" or "**condemnor**".

3.
The Condemnation Process:
A Step-by-Step Flowchart

The following is a flowchart of the steps in the eminent domain condemnation process in Texas, followed by a more detailed explanation of each step:

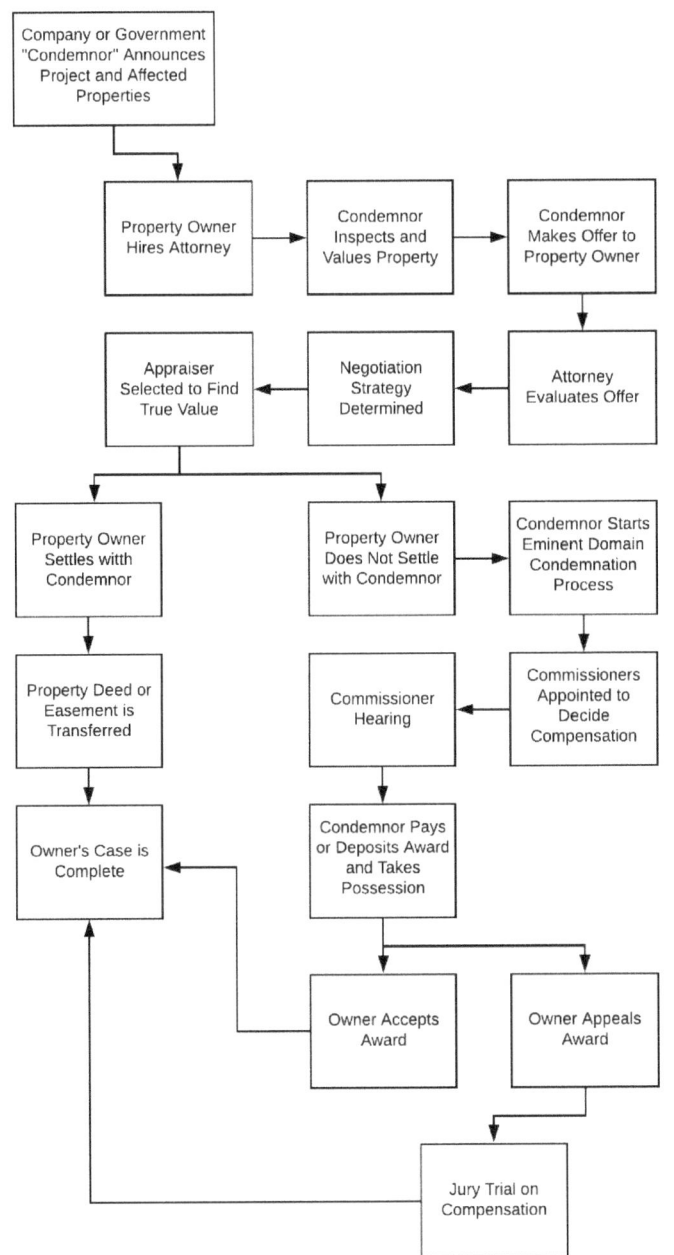

4.
Condemnation Steps:
The Details

1. Company or Government "Condemnor" Announces Project and Affected Properties

Often during project development, the condemning authority will hold public meetings to notify the public of the upcoming project and how this project will affect private property. Private companies must follow certain procedures to be granted eminent domain authority to take land for projects. The entity that wants to take your property using the legal process of eminent domain condemnation is called the "condemnor".

2. Property Owner Hires Attorney
An eminent domain lawyer should be hired as soon as possible to help guide the process and negotiate the best settlement for the landowner. Depending upon the complexity of the case, the value of the property and the amount of damages to any remaining property, it may be necessary to allow condemnation to occur in order for the property owner to receive fair compensation. If this is the case, an eminent domain lawyer should always be hired to assist the property owner with their claim.

3. Condemnor Inspects and Values Property

Before the condemning authority makes an offer, they must determine the value of the property being taken, and all damages associated with the taking. This valuation is determined by an appraiser and then reviewed by the condemning authority before an offer is made. These appraisers often have long-standing relationships with the condemnor and want to keep project costs low so they keep getting hired by the condemnor for more appraisals. These appraisals may contain errors such as using incorrect comparable properties, or they may not value your property at its "highest and best use". Frequently, they ignore severance issues or dramatically understate their significance and impact.

4. Condemnor Makes Offer to Property Owner

The condemning authority must provide the property owner a copy of the Texas Landowner's Bill of Rights. The condemning authority must disclose with the offer any and all existing appraisal reports produced or acquired by the condemnor relating to the owner's property and used in determining the final valuation offer.

5. Attorney Evaluates Offer

After the condemning authority makes an offer, the property owner's attorney will evaluate the appraisal and offer to determine if it represents just compensation. If the attorney finds errors in the condemnor's valuation, then they will determine how best to proceed.

6. Negotiation Strategy Determined
The attorney will need to assess all damages that were not included in the condemnor's valuation and determine the full amount of compensation owed to the property owner. The attorney will then determine how best to present this information to the condemning authority during the negotiation phase.

7. Appraiser Selected to Find True Value
In many eminent domain cases, a second appraisal must be conducted on the property in order to determine the full value owed to the landowner, including those missed by the condemning authority's appraiser. This appraisal is submitted as evidence supporting the property owner's claim for additional compensation. A property owner must disclose to the condemning authority any and all appraisal reports produced or acquired by the property owner relating specifically to the owner's property and used in determining the owner's opinion of value. It is highly recommended to consult with an eminent domain attorney prior to obtaining a second appraisal. Any and all appraisals done on the property to determine the owner's opinion of the value must be submitted to the condemning authority.

If you hire an appraiser on your own who is not experienced in valuing property in eminent domain cases, you may end up with an appraisal that contains errors that will be used against you in court. Hiring a wrong appraiser can seriously jeopardize a good claim. An eminent domain attorney will thoroughly review the initial appraisal and determine its strengths and weaknesses. Based on this information, the attorney will indicate a selection for the most qualified appraiser to value the property in question and determine the damages to any remaining land. Make sure you consult with an eminent domain attorney before hiring an appraiser on your own.

8. Property Owner Settles with Condemnor
If the property owner is satisfied with the offer they can sign the final settlement papers and give up their right to pursue additional damages. At that point the case is complete.

9. Deed or Easement is Transferred
Once the final settlement papers are signed by the property owner, the deed or easement is transferred to the condemnor. It is at this time that ownership is transferred from the property owner to the condemning authority.

10. Owner's Case is Complete
The owner is paid in full, the condemning authority owns the property, and the owner's case is finished. The

property owner can no longer file a claim to challenge the taking or to receive additional compensation.

11. Property Owner Does Not Settle with Condemnor
If the property owner is not satisfied with the amount offered by the condemning authority they can refuse the offer and allow condemnation to occur.

12. Condemnor Starts Eminent Domain Condemnation Process
If the condemning authority cannot reach a settlement agreement with the property owner, they may begin the condemnation proceedings by filing a petition in the proper court. The condemnor does this by filing a civil lawsuit for condemnation of the property.

13. Commissioners Appointed to Decide Compensation
The judge in the court where the condemnation petition was filed or to which an eminent domain case is assigned will appoint three disinterested landowners who reside in the county as special commissioners to determine the amount that should be paid to the owner whose land is being taken.

14. Commissioner Hearing
The special commissioners schedule a hearing where each party may present their evidence supporting their opinion on the amount of damages and just compensation. The special commissioners will admit evidence of 1. the value of the property being

condemned, 2. the injury to the property owner, 3. the benefit to the property owner's remaining property; and 4. the use of the property for the purpose of the condemnation. The commissioners then come up with an amount to be awarded to the landowner.

15. Condemnor Pays or Deposits Award and Takes Possession

After the special commissioners have made an award in the eminent domain proceeding, the condemning authority can usually take possession of the property, provided the condemning authority pays the property owner the amount of damages and costs awarded by the special commissioners or deposits that amount of money with the court. If the money is deposited with the court, the property owner can petition the court to withdrawal the money. Prior to withdrawing the money, the owner must file a tax certificate from the tax collector for each taxable parcel on the condemned property showing that there are no delinquent taxes, penalties, interest, or costs owed on the condemned property or on any larger tract of which the condemned property forms a part. At the time of acquisition the condemnor will give the property owner notice that the owner and the owner's heirs are entitled to repurchase the property if the public use for which the property was acquired through eminent domain is canceled before the 10th anniversary of the date of acquisition. The repurchase price is the fair market value of the property at the time the public use was canceled.

16. Owner Accepts Commissioner Award as Final
If the owner is satisfied with the amount of compensation determined by the special commissioners, they may agree to the award, therefore waiving their right to pursue additional just compensation and their case is done.

17. Owner Appeals Commissioner Award
If the property owner is not satisfied with the amount of just compensation as determined by the special commissioners, they can appeal this award by filing a formal objection. This objection must be filed within the legal deadline after the commissioner hearing or it is waived. Note that the condemnor can also file an objection to the award if they believe it was unfair and wish to proceed with regular litigation.

18. Jury Trial on Compensation
If the objection is filed, a trial will be conducted in the same manner as other civil cases to determine the amount of damages and just compensation.

5.
Right-of-Way Agents:
Tricks of the Trade

I received a call from a client whose mother lives on a ranch out in the country. A large corporation wanted to run a pipeline right through the middle of her property. The folks negotiating with my client's mom had interacted with her in a way that her son didn't feel was honest or forthright. He felt his mother was being bullied. He asked me to take a look at her situation and provide my legal opinion. But first, I had to provide my human opinion. Simply put, no one should be treated this way.

Before I explain why experiences like these are fairly common, I want to explain how eminent domain condemnation negotiations work. For example, when a company wants to create a natural gas pipeline that snakes across Texas, they need to negotiate with landowners to get easements for the pipeline. To do this, they hire what are known as right-of-way agents. These are people tasked with securing the land rights for a project. While they represent the pipeline company's interests, they are usually independent contractors hired for this specific purpose.

The right-of-way agent's goal is to get your land as quickly and cheaply as possible so that the pipeline company will continue using them for these projects. The agent may be friendly, but they are not your friend. Their best interest is the opposite of yours. Agents are under pressure to resolve issues quickly and for as little money as possible. That pressure can force some of these agents to be less than truthful or use underhanded manipulation to get your signature.

In my dealings with right-of-way agents in eminent domain cases, I've seen certain negotiating tricks used over and over. One method is to misrepresent how long you as a property owner have to make a decision. "You have two weeks to accept an offer," the agent may say. "After that, we'll need to begin court proceedings." They say this to create anxiety and urgency in your mind and put you under pressure. The agent's statement may be true, but it might not. Either way, you should not take the agent's word for it. Projects and court proceedings can take time. By law, there are certain built-in time periods the condemning authority must provide to allow the landowner to evaluate the offer for their property.

Another common trick could best be described as "everybody's doing it" or "last man standing." An agent may tell you that all your neighbors have agreed to a settlement and you are the "last holdout." Most landowners have no idea if this is true or not unless they communicate regularly with all their neighbors. Again, the goal of the agent is simply to rush the landowner into agreeing to a deal, regardless of the owner's best interests. Also, remember that every property is different and what your neighbor agreed to may be irrelevant to the value you deserve for your property. Besides, your neighbor may have made a bad deal!

Finally, agents may discourage you from calling an attorney, telling you it will only create hassle and cost you money. This is not true. For example, in the cases we accept at our firm, we work on a contingency basis, where we only get paid if we get you more than the first offer you receive from the other side. If we do, then we are paid a percentage of the additional money above the original offer. And, if we don't get you more than the initial offer, we don't get paid. This allows you to get expert legal representation without having to pay any up-front legal fees and without "going backward" from the offer you already have. The vast majority of landowners do not obtain full value for their property because they do not get help from an eminent domain condemnation lawyer. Obviously, right of way agents won't tell you any of this because it saves them from having to pay full value for your land.

Knowing all this, what should you as a landowner do to protect yourself? First, educate yourself about the condemnation process by reading the rest of this guide. Then contact an eminent domain attorney as soon as you learn about a project affecting your property or hear from a right-of-way agent.

6.
Terms of an Easement:
Look Beyond the Money

In many cases, the government or a private company wants to use only part of your land for their project, rather than your entire property. The document they draft that details the terms of their agreement with you is called an "easement". Understanding what an easement is, how it works, and what to watch out for will go a long way towards providing you peace of mind about the condemnation process.

An easement is a contract detailing how and why a condemnor will use your land and how they will compensate you. Technically speaking, an easement doesn't give full ownership of the land to the entity using it. Instead, it gives them the right to use that land under the conditions specified. This condition, called a right-of-way, is usually granted on a permanent basis, which means you need to be sure you are getting the best possible terms before you sign any deal. You won't get a chance to renegotiate or alter terms years down the road, so you have to get it right the first time.

As an eminent domain attorney, I've learned most people aren't aware of what to look out for and what to ask for in an easement. And the sad truth is this situation just how the companies that create these documents like it. A right-of-way agent may point you to specific provisions in the easement, assuring you it's what you hoped for, but you should never sign an easement without thoroughly reading it for yourself and having an attorney review it. There's too much at stake to simply take the agent's word for it.

The biggest mistake I see people make when it comes to assessing an easement is only looking at the dollar value offered. How much money you'll receive is important, but so are the terms. How will the project builder protect your land during construction? If they will be digging up your land, how will they restore it? What happens if they damage a power line or water well while working? Will they provide fencing and other structures to clearly mark where the project is running and to protect livestock and other assets? If a pipe ruptures and damages land not covered in the easement, how will you be compensated? These are just some of the things to consider in an easement. You have to be willing to analyze the document from all sides to determine whether you should sign the agreement. And again, you only get one chance to do it right.

The company handling the easement may try to persuade you to not work with an attorney. They know clients who consult lawyers receive better easement terms and more money, even after paying their attorney, than those who try to do it themselves. In some cases, the price you're paid for an easement may go up while the agreement actually becomes less valuable to you due to other easement clauses disappearing. Situations like these are exactly why it's best to speak with a condemnation lawyer as early as possible.

7.
The Condemnation Appraiser:
An Essential Investment

When you are facing the loss of all or part of your land in eminent domain condemnation, the most important thing you can do to protect your right to full compensation, after hiring an eminent domain attorney, is to hire a qualified eminent domain appraiser.

The condemnation process is a battle of experts. The corporation or government entity that wants to take your land always has an appraiser as their expert. The appraisal they create is they key evidence they will use to get your property and pay you as little money as possible. Their appraiser has an incentive to "low-ball" the value of your land in order to keep the condemning authority happy and continue to get hired to do more project appraisals. They will present their appraisal in the formal offer your receive, at the special commissioners' hearing and also in court. If you attend any type of hearing without your own appraiser and your own appraisal report as evidence, you are essentially "unarmed" in the battle for your land.

It is vital to have your own appraisal done as early in the process as possible. It is equally important that you use an appraiser that has experience in eminent domain appraisals. Unlike a normal appraiser, eminent domain appraisers have experience in determining the "highest and best use" for your property. This translates into more money for you for both the value of what is being taken and, in the case of a partial taking, the value of the damages to any remaining property, which can sometimes be the largest part of the compensation. Eminent domain appraisers also have experience in presenting their evidence in a convincing way at the special commissioners' hearing and in court. Also, having a solid appraisal to back up your demand increases your chances of settling your case without going to court.

Although eminent domain appraisals can be expensive, the additional value they add to your case will almost always far outweigh the cost. Many landowners are surprised at how much their land is actually worth and what they should be paid for a condemnation taking. If you are serious about maximizing the amount of money you receive for what is being taken from you, hiring an experienced condemnation appraiser is an essential investment. Your eminent domain attorney will advise you in picking the right one for your case.

8.
Special Commissioners' Hearing:
A Unique Aspect of Condemnation

Texas eminent domain condemnation is a peculiar process. One unusual feature is the special commissioner hearing. Here's how it works. The government or a private company wants to use all or a portion of your land for a public project. To do so, they first are required to try and reach a settlement agreement with you. A right-of-way agent contacts you, offers you a price, and hopes you'll accept it. If you don't reach an agreement, the company will sue you in hopes of settling the matter in court. Before that court date can happen, though, your case will go to a special commissioner hearing.

Rather than being presided over by a judge, the hearing is run by the special commissioners. The commissioners are a panel of three landowners from the county where your land is who are appointed by the court. At the hearing, each side has a chance to explain their position and then the commissioners decide on a settlement figure. If either side rejects the commissioners' conclusion, the claim moves into the courts.

The commissioners do not have to be lawyers and do not have to possess any previous experience with eminent domain law. Although they are supposed to be neutral, the appointed commissioners tend to see the same attorney representing the condemning authority (the one taking your property) over and over again, while they may only meet the landowner and their lawyer for the first time at a hearing. This can lead some commissioners to favor the condemning authority over the landowner. Combined with the unequal resources of each side (the company behind the project has lots of lawyers and lots of money to fight to get your property for the lowest possible amount) this favoritism can make the special commissioner hearing process a true David and Goliath situation, with you in the role of David.

Remember that the company seeking an easement always wants to get you to accept the lowest possible offer. If you're not careful, a special commissioner hearing can enable them to do just that. Working with an attorney who understands the ins and outs of the process is your best chance to level the playing field and achieve a great outcome. You should at least discuss your case and your options with an eminent domain attorney as soon as possible, and you should never go to a special commissioner hearing without legal representation.

To give you a sense of just how arcane this process is, one of my clients at a recent hearing was an attorney himself with years of litigation experience. But with no experience in the strange world of eminent domain law, he sought me out to represent him. If somebody with a law degree knows they need help when it comes to handling a condemnation case, it goes without saying that people with no legal training should also get help from an eminent domain attorney.

9.
Hire a Condemnation Lawyer: Your Key to Success

When you discover that the government or a private company wants to take your land to build a new pipeline, transmission line, or highway, after the initial shock wears off, you may wonder if you need to hire a lawyer to help you. You may think "Why not do it myself so I keep more of the money?" But, in the case of eminent domain, hiring an attorney is almost always a better way to end up with more money, even after the attorney is paid. And having representation makes the process a lot easier and less stressful for you.

Most people have not dealt with eminent domain condemnation before. They may understand the concept without understanding how the process works. Whoever is taking your land thrives in this situation because they know the process very well and how to "work the system" to your disadvantage. They know how to manipulate the situation in their favor, using time pressure, ignorance of the process and fear of an uncertain outcome to get you to accept an unfair amount for your property. Experience and research play large roles in securing reasonable compensation, but it is unlikely you will have the time or ability to seek either before your land is seized.

To level this playing field, you need an experienced ally on your side. While the initial offer for your land might seem reasonable to you, an attorney can put everything into perspective, including costs and compensations you may not have considered.

Your attorney can advise you when to enlist outside experts, such as appraisers, land use experts or engineers to help you determine how a project may harm your land and what your property is really worth. Your lawyer will also help you seek compensation for "damages to the remainder" when only a portion of your property is taken.

Having an experienced eminent domain lawyer representing you signals to the condemnor that you know your rights and are willing to fight to make them pay full compensation and provide fair terms in the agreement that will protect you and your property.

Being represented by counsel also lets whoever is taking your property know that you are willing to go to court if necessary in order to be treated fairly. Ironically, this preparation and willingness to push back against an unfair offer often leads to cases settling sooner for more money without having to go to court.

10.
How We Can Help:
Why You Should Contact Us Now

Todd Law Firm provides the knowledge and experience you need to get maximum compensation for your land. We act as a buffer between you and the condemning authority, allowing you to focus on your work and your family while your rights are being protected.

With our "No Win No Fee" guarantee, we only get paid if we win by getting you more money than the first offer you receive for your land. Our fee is a percentage of that increased amount so you can receive expert help with no up-front fees and without "going backward" from your current offer.

Don't wait. Projects can move quickly and deadlines affect your case. If you're facing eminent domain condemnation, get the support you need to maximize your compensation and protect your rights. To discuss your case and learn how we can help, contact us now at **(512) 472-7799** or **davidtoddlaw.com**.

Todd Law Firm
Eminent Domain Condemnation
Protecting Texas Landowners
3800 N. Lamar Blvd., Ste. 200, Austin, TX 78756
ph: (512) 472-7799
davidtoddlaw.com

About the Author

Eminent domain attorney David Todd specializes in protecting commercial and large-tract landowners in corporate and government condemnation cases throughout Texas. He has been selected as a Texas Super Lawyer every year since 2014 and is a member of the Multi-Million Dollar Advocates Forum.

www.ingramcontent.com/pod-product-compliance
Lightning Source LLC
Chambersburg PA
CBHW040258220526
45473CB00002B/523